DANCE
DANCE
REVOLUTION

THE BARNARD WOMEN POETS PRIZE

Edited by Saskia Hamilton

2003
Figment
Rebecca Wolff
Chosen by Eavan Boland and Claudia Rankine

2004
The Return Message
Tessa Rumsey
Chosen by Jorie Graham

2005
Orient Point
Julie Sheehan
Chosen by Linda Gregg

2006
Dance Dance Revolution
Cathy Park Hong
Chosen by Adrienne Rich

BARNARD WOMEN POETS PRIZE CITATION
BY ADRIENNE RICH

"*Dance Dance Revolution* is a poem-sequence in two voices: 'The Guide' is a former South Korean dissident from the Kwangju uprising of 1980 (comparable to Tianenmen Square, brutally repressed with the support of the U.S.) She speaks a fluid international language called Desert Creole, which draws, the poem tells us, from 300 emigré language groups including Spanish Caribbean patois, Asian 'pidgin,' Latin, German and Middle English. She is interviewed by 'The Historian,' a scholar raised in Sierra Leone, who annotates the Guide's commentaries in Standard English. There is a personal connection between the two, which is gradually revealed. The interviews take place in a planned city called The Desert (reminiscent of Dubai or Las Vegas) where replicas of major world cities have been built as tourist resorts, offering every luxury. The Guide has ended up, after her release from political prison, as a tourist guide in the St. Petersburg Hotel. The time of the poem is 2016.

"The mixture of imagination, language and historical consciousness in this book is marvelous. The Guide speaks as one of those migrant people the world over whose past has been ruptured or erased by political violence, who plays whatever role she must in the world of the global economy, using language as subversion and disguise. Her speech mocks, threatens and beguiles, shifting back and forth from lyrical and elegiac to visceral and satiric. The poems spoken by the Guide are interlaced with 'excerpts from the Historian's Memoir' in Standard English. Thus the rich, allusive texture of the Desert Creole is set in high relief, while two very different life-stories unfold.

"Hong's work is passionate, artful, worldly. It makes a reader feel and think simultaneously, and rather than implying a nihilistic or negative vision of the future, it leaves this reader, at least, revitalized. To quote from an early passage in the Historian's voice: *Revolutions exist in time capsules. . . . The pulse of unrest works unpredictably, in canny acts of sabotage.* As it works here."

—Adrienne Rich, Barnard Women Poets Prize citation

ALSO BY CATHY PARK HONG

Translating Mo'um

DANCE
DANCE
REVOLUTION

poems

Cathy Park Hong

W. W. Norton & Company New York London

For information about permission to reproduce selections from this book, write to Permissions, W. W. Norton & Company, Inc., 500 Fifth Avenue, New York, NY 10110

Manufacturing by Courier Westford
Book design by Anna Oler

Library of Congress Cataloging-in-Publication Data

Hong, Cathy Park.
Dance dance revolution : poems / Cathy Park Hong. — 1st ed.
p. cm.
ISBN 978-0-393-06484-1 (hardcover)
1. Korean Americans—Poetry. I. Title.
PS3608.O494438D36 2007
811'.6—dc22   2007002386

W. W. Norton & Company, Inc.
500 Fifth Avenue, New York, N.Y. 10110
www.wwnorton.com

W. W. Norton & Company Ltd.
Castle House, 75/76 Wells Street, London W1T 3QT

1 2 3 4 5 6 7 8 9 0

To my sister Nancy

ACKNOWLEDGEMENTS

To Adrienne Rich, with my deepest gratitude.

To the editors of the following publications, in which excerpts of *Dance Dance Revolution* have previously appeared, some in earlier versions: *Denver Quarterly*, *American Letters and Commentary*, *McSweeney's*, *Action Yes*, *Canary*, *Verse*, *Volt*, and *Chain*.

To friends and teachers who have provided support and much-needed input toward this book: Ghita Schwartz, Shannon Welch, Jen Liu, Malena Watrous, Liz Goodman, Bonnie Jones, Cal Bedient, Mark Levine, Cole Swensen, and James Galvin. A special thank-you to my W. W. Norton editor, Jill Bialosky, and her assistant, Evan Carver.

To the MacDowell Colony, the New York Foundation for the Arts fellowship, and National Endowment for the Arts grant, without which I never would have finished this book.

To my beloved family and to Mores McWreath, for his patience and amazing support.

CONTENTS

CHRONOLOGY OF THE DESERT GUIDE

1960   Born in a small town near Kwangju, South Korea.
        President Syngman Rhee steps down.
        Her mother, a famous Pansori singer, dies.

1969   Diagnosed with a rare disease that prevents hair growth.

1974   Moves out of her father's house and lives with her
        teacher.

1978   Attends University to study political science and English.
        Falls in love with Kim Yoon-Sah, another key activist of
        the Kwangju uprising.

1979   Her father dies of an unknown illness.

1980   South Korean government taken over by a military coup
        led by Chun Du-Hwan.
        Helps foment an uprising against the coup.
        One of few survivors of the Ginseng Colony.

1983   Moves to the Desert. Works as a housekeeper at the
        Paris Hotel.

1988   Year of Dance Dance Revolution, an uprising fomented
        by native residents. They are exiled to New Town,
        located along the borders of the Desert.

1989   Becomes a junior hotel tour guide at the St. Petersburg
        Hotel.

1990   Quits and works as a guide for Belgrade Inn.

1992   Returns to St. Petersburg Hotel after Belgrade Inn
        closes down.

1998   Briefly marries and divorces a fellow guide.

2005   Increased deaths from land mine accidents. Tourism
        industry falls by 30 percent.

2016   Appointed senior guide of the St. Petersburg Hotel.

FOREWORD

In the Desert, the language is an amalgam of some three hundred languages and dialects imported into this city, a rapidly evolving lingua franca. The language, while borrowing the inner structures of English grammar, also borrows from existing and extinct English dialects. Here, new faces pour in and civilian accents morph so quickly that their accents betray who they talked to that day rather than their cultural roots. Fluency is also a matter of opinion. There is no tuning fork to one's twang. Still, dialects differ greatly depending on region. In the Southern Region, they debate whether they should even call their language English since it has transformed so completely as to be rendered unrecognizable from its origin. As an example, I have included a brief conversation I overheard at the hotel bar:

1. Dimfo me am im.
Let me tell you about him.

2. Burblim frum' im
He said

3. Wit blodhued mout,
with his red mouth (or bloody mouth)

4. G'won now, shi'bal bato
Leave, you homosexual son of a baboon.

5. So din he lip dim clout.
So then he punched him in the mouth.

6. Bar goons hoistim off. Exeunt.
Security escorted him out of the bar.

You will find that the customer at the bar speaks in a thicker brogue while the tour guide interviewed for this book has a more expansive vocabulary. I suspect that in the guide's line of work, she gathers slang, idioms, and argot from other tour guides and tourists (which does not explain her use of the Middle English).

I've had difficulty deciding whether to transcribe her words exactly as said or to translate it to a more "standard" English. I decided on a compromise—preserving her diction in certain sections while translating her words to a proper English when I felt clarification was needed. I must also admit that some of her stories may be inexact due to technical glitches. During one unfortunate day, I left my cassette tapes out in my patio during a rainstorm. It has not caused irreparable damage but the static has obscured parts of the recording so there may be some lapses in her testimonials. I have marked such lapses with ellipses.

Overall, the Desert is the planned city of renewed wonders, city of state-of-the-art hotels modeled after the world's greatest cities, city whose decree is *there is difference only in degree*. This city is the center of elsewhere but perhaps that is not accurate. As the world shrinks, elsewhere begins to disappear.

Revolutions happen all the time elsewhere, although we seem to think that revolutions exist in time capsules. Back then, they were an act of propulsion, of anguished, woodcut masses marching in cohesion. Now in the Desert, the pulse of unrest works unpredictably, in canny acts of sabotage engineered by exiled natives who crave for time to stand still. Here, rumors abound that migrant hotel employees are now joining them and tourists don't know who to trust. The city of rest is also the city of unrest.

I am a historian who arrived here to hear about a different unrest. A place once considered elsewhere: Kwangju. Kwangju is the provincial capital in the southern part of South Korea. After a dictatorial takeover in 1980, the citizens of Kwangju rose up to protest the coup, only to be brutally massacred by the U.S.-backed Korean government. My father, who later moved on to become a physician for Doctors Without Borders in Sierra Leone, was part of that protest. But even to his death, he revealed nothing about his past life. And my own mother, a shy Midwestern woman, died before I turned three. I am a historian, you see, but history has always been stingy to me.

Then I discovered that she moved to the Desert after Kwangju. The woman my father loved before my mother. The woman whose pirated radio station led thousands into the streets during the uprising. "Her radio speeches were pure and hypnotic in their urgency for us to rise up against the regime," said one civilian. My guide.

I slipped out of the airport's sliding doors and squinted in the late afternoon sun. I could not make out any form, only refracted lobes of sunlight and the shadow flittings of tourists who just arrived. Then, wearing a ginger-colored wig and a navy pin-striped suit, she emerged out of an air-conditioned town car and invited me in. I pressed my recorder. On the hour-long ride to the hotel, she was silent until the remains of my tape squealed to its end. She then smiled, clasped my hand, and gave me a complimentary swim cap. When I puzzled over this gift, she hushed my question. She will give me a tour first. She introduced herself. "Chun Sujin, lest name first, first name lest. Allatime known es Ballhead, Jangnim, o zoologist Henrietta wit falsetto slang. But you, you jus' call me guide."

I

STROLLING THROUGH
THE HOTEL

ROLES

. . . Opal o opus,
behole, neon hibiscus bloom beacons!
"Tan Lotion Tanya" billboard . . . she
your lucent Virgil, den I's taka ova
as talky Virgil . . . want some tea? Some pelehuu?

Mine vocation your vacation!
. . . I train mine talk box to talk yep-puh, as you
'Merikkens say "purdy," no goods only phrases,
betta de phrase, "purdier" de experience,

twenty t'ousand guides here but I'm #1 . . .
once, Helsinkian arrive, I's say "I guide I guide"
but Helsinkian yap "No! Too many guides!" den I sleep outside
'im door, 'im wake, I say calmly "I guide"
y Helsinkian say "Goddammunt, ja okay, guide me!"

. . . a million lightbulbs en Desert wit cleanest latrines
en our strobe lit lobbies since desert non sin . . . each
hotel de McCosm o any city . . . Bangkok ova here,
Paree ova dere . . .

I speak sum Han-guk y Finnish, good bit o Latin
y Spanish . . . sum toto Desert Creole en evachanging dipdong
'pendable on mine mood . . . ibid . . .

. . . Many 'Merikken dumplings unhinge dim
talk holes y ejaculate *oooh* y *hot-diggity*,
dis is de *shee-it* . . . but gut ripping done to erect Polis,
we expoit gaggle o aborigini to back tundra county . . .
Bannitus! But betta to scrape dat fact
unda history rug, so shh . . .

O tempora, O mores! I usta move
around like Innuit lookim for sea pelt . . . now
I'mma double migrant. Ceded from Koryo, ceded from
'Merikka, ceded y ceded until now I seizem
dis sizable Mouthpiece role . . . now les' drive to interior.

ST. PETERSBURG HOTEL SERIES

1. SERVICES

See radish turrets stuck wit tumor lights around hotel
lika glassblown Russki castle sans Pinko plight,
only Ebsolute voodka fountains. Gaggle fo drink?

Hundred ruble, cold kesh only. Step up y molest
hammer y chicklets studded en ruby y seppire almost
bling badda bling. Question? No question! Prick ear.

Coroner diagnose hotel as king o hotels 'cos luxury
is eberyting. Hear sound speaker sing "I get laid in me Escalade
but I first sip glass of Cristal / den I whip out me pistol."

Non worry. No pistol en hotel, only best surgeon fish y beluga
bedtime special. Deelicious. But before you tuck en king o
water bed, befo you watch pay-pa-view,

Be peripatetic y behole snow bears merry en a ball o go
be roused bine molten sauna where Babushkas bap your tush
wit boar bristle switch. No chillins allowed, vide kid. Mo mo?

Blood rust has been Windexed to amber shine,
insurrecta's marauding soul wetted into papa-machetes,
looted radio back en turtle-doved municipal hands.

Here, city o ebening calm, ignis-rilers gone.
If you want true history, go watch tailor y milna
make magic. Dim more revolutionary den artist.

If you dream fo Paris, Paris Hotel right outside
atrium, beyond sand dunes, which form y disappear
like mekkinations o human digestion. Sand swirl

to otherworld land where blankets de weight o human
bodies tatter y pill. No tatting, no pilling here. Sand will
be en your eye, only sometimes.

Note from the Historian
Asked why she chose to be a guide at the St. Petersburg Hotel, she replied that
it was her calling to work as a guide for the great hotel of St. Petersburg and
besides, her heritage and the heritage of Russians are similar: they both love
the combination of dried fish and very strong liquor.

2. PREPARATION FOR WINTER IN THE ST. PETERSBURG ARBORETUM

Gardenas clip leaves, mow down calla lilies
wit petrol-gunning motocade, sling slenda pile
o white trumpet lilies ova shoulders,
herd piddisnip flowas away like blighted damsels.

Now Gardena squad weavil glass y dews en trees.
Icim trees fo winta's memorial.
Lika beachwood sheltas' wind chimes,
de branch branch *clinkity-clank* wit ice.

Now samsy, grab un gun. BB down de riving ravens,
de vermin fatted jays, y jade headed mallards who wit
insolence nest en botany o our #3 prize-winnim plants,
who dare nest en hearts o Russkies sculpt en shrubbery.

G'won now, shoot! I's look at me wrist clock, almost Deciembre,
sap a bloodgout ooze en fall but en winta,
trees mus' be spare lika balsam pim peck.
Origini yaar? So we vacuum sap wit a cleva—

Oi, oi! Mifela Gardena! You half bark up a tree
en wrong location, it be dat tree you chop!
Now samsy, les' be avid again. Ah! Seasons chenji,
green turns mint, now, g'won wit de gun.

Ahoy! Whitening wadder fountain. Drink. Afta cuppa-ful
o aqua vitae, yo pissin fang transfomate to puh'ly whites
lika Bollywood actress swole en saffron,
flashim her tarta molar to she coquetry man.

I'se drink gallon-a-day . . . (*bares her teeth*) ssshhhee?
Issshh beautiful, eh? . . . Frum purim H_2O wit fluoride
y sulfate y tu typical humectant lika xylitol
which supa-boosta fluoride's cavity fightim powa.

So g'won miff, you mus' drink. Me good-fo-nut'ing
fadder once ses to me, "*Ttalim*, you mus' hab whitest
teef so you catchim holistic hotshot man." Ipsi dixit!
Mine fadder hed rat-hole teef, y you hab it too wit dim
nicotine mold en dim pachyderm tusk.

Eberyone hab bes' teef! Shinier den 'Merikken
Colgates . . . 'Cos mine molar, I'se attract lusty lubbas,
but I non lustim if dim have moss sweaters en teef
even if dim wining dining me. As mine fadder ses,
"You triumph only wit de whitest."

4. THE WASHROOMS OF ST. PETERSBURG

Behole de toilet gurgle o flush kaputs en zip second,
de porcelite not clam cold but warm lika
oven-loin mits . . . urging ye waste to dive
into cleanest ammonio pond.

De boottons en toilet manifold! Pequeno
es mung beans: one fo concierge if ye suffrin
belly-ache, nutt'a squirts a fountain o
wadder to wash ye besmirched hole afta satis,
one dat vill pipe en Wagna o disco, din parfum
to fume de offal air.

So comfy, gratus latrines maki ye wanna sit
en its porcelite domus y read great lititure . . .
Mind ova matta samsy, mind ova matta, even if ye ate
bad Mulligatawny, ye mind's fog will curdle
to clearest tought balloon.

Reflect en *hows* y *whys* en de day's events.
O tink, fist proppim chin, bout Being—yes, sentient
being, ye may ponder, sense o essence?

O ye may muse back ebening befo,
en blue-lumen Lounge, when ye hed sensual tension
wit tenderone lass, whist ye knees be kissim neat' de table.

31

Toilets so seductive, ye tush
vacuumed to hole, stuck lika fire ant trapped
innim own feast o glaceed peach pie.

5. ATOP THE ST. PETERSBURG DOME

De ebening es mine, starry as himbo's
bubble, de ebening wit stars en grid, starry ya?
Stars ideation en dome, me vocal twills in dome, listen—
HULLO . . . hullo . . . hullo . . .

Vaulted up y up, we reach ad astra,
ad astra we reach . . . no conflict o war
en de desert, no rat-a-tat per se . . .

once unrest shatta'd desert horizon to ellipses,
haunted slay de flames feasted de hotels y sommelier,
feasted de lawn foliage y swim-pool,
y char de head chumps to Malaga raisins.

When I'se comeupon fo tippame-turban job,
greyhound dogs, spectas en dawn fog,
traipse de trash-boil mountains fo scrap cook pork,
nut'ing left but scrap metal y bitterness . . .
I de frosh guide maki pennies 'cos no one *ooh-aaahing*.

I guided misbegodder fool who vacation
en woebegone ruins. Tu, I mean, you tryim.
To flower-arrange words so sand-piss
ash sounds like *Melodious plot of
beechen green*, try, nary!

No money cash flow fo me 'cos no foliage, no
va-va-va-boom sites to show. . . . I'se lika white fes mime,
gesturim atta air en actu . . . a game show lass
wit no appliance to show . . .

So I makeum up gammon, no goodfela am me,
I makeum up . . . Am I yesman like mine fadder y grandfadder?
Am I mimas hucksta? O dolus doldrum. Mine
dome skin red-alert from wig rash.
I's leave you be. Mus' exeunt.

Note from the Historian
After the guide inexplicably abandoned me, I was forced to entertain myself.
For hours, I wandered through St. Petersburg's many rooms, stopping by the
bar for a shot of onion flavored vodka while listening to *Swan Lake* (which
they play on loop) and then ended up in a lounge, where I was relieved to find
her again.

KARAOKE LOUNGE

Impish peeper, impish peeper, you ear-dropping?
When I ululate til mine fes a grapey pulp,
croaking K-pop en dis privacy-room? Me bumming,
see? Shoo, *ga*, tour is ova, scug . . .
Shoo . . .

Non . . . no, stay. Stay,
Some sing swallow nightingales. *Ahem* . . .
phlegm, some sing swallow nightingale en agora,
but we closet singas en a box,

a mike—a grog sodden salary man sing, "O lore,
no harem, jus' mefelf," he keens, til he lurch
into him mike wit no invocatory might, him lung
raisined like him balls, he sleepim, dreaming o
tong-il o *tigers in red weather* . . .

We sing solo, tone-deaf,
gargle a bauble, it pops dead o night . . .
Anon, Sinatra canon . . . Aska ballad bloom
en room din buzza stop,
So ye want to hear me story? Ab initio?
'Bout mine domus, 'bout Sah?

Mine madder, rest her soul, sang fo all,
lung a fireplace breatha, bronchial tree aflame til she spit
a blood wad, she sang pansori, one beat
drum a ko bell. Whole day a story sung, tong-seung!

Aiiiree . . . Airreee . . . epic song lasting
twotreefo day . . . sponge up de Han . . . ssulp'un yaegge . . .
Ssarang-han nam'pyun . . . wit only a fan y jug to wet her troat . . .

Despite the rumblings of a civil war in Freetown, Sierra Leone, I spent most of my childhood in quiet solitude. I owned dozens of cookie tins filled with crayons and whiled my days drawing pictures in a sitting room with egg-white walls and a slowly rotating ceiling fan. I was a peaceful, oblivious child with only one true anxiety: the burden of consciousness. I had difficulty understanding why I—my mind, my consciousness—was in one body and not another. Did others possess the same kind of *command* and awareness over themselves? Were they just chattering machines without the gift of inner thought? I concluded that consciousness was a cursed, supernatural power that only I possessed and I had to keep it secret. I attended an international primary school and I remember watching a short film about an animated mole with my class. The film reel stuttered along and my classmate, Michel, whispered to me: "I will tell you a secret if you tell me a secret." He quickly whispered his and then asked for mine. In my most solemn tone, I replied, "I can't. It's too big a secret. I can't even begin to tell you."

II

STIRRINGS OF CHILDHOOD
THAT BEGIN WITH

SONG THAT BREAKS THE WORLD RECORD

. . . I's born en first day o unrest . . .
Huzza de students who fightim plisboi patos!
En gangrene smoke, youngins t'rew butane Colas,
chanted por ole cantanka Rhee to step down . . . he did!
Chased out en a perma holiday,
Hawaii him Elba . . .

Fizzy ale spillim street, Korea celebring . . .
No money fo balloon swine y ticka-tape parade
but Koreans hab unabashed national succotash . . .
Whole country batty drunk, carpe cerevisi,
aroused like itchy Veegra man . . .

All b'mine madder . . . Alore, drunk medics swished
out clinics to celebre, so she allim sheself . . . alone
en hospital yowlim frum labor . . . but expert she is,
bore ten chillins whom all die befo
reachim age one . . . (her heart a grave
o infants, me tragic mum)

. . . breat' she pansori's breath . . . lika fire
breatha accordian, dum spiro, spero . . . y

pop me out . . . (me yeller fadder
hid home, hidim from froth o birth's labor

y labor o revolution). . . . I'se boomerang
out, slip shod onto blood tile floor . . .
a squalim bile newborn . . .

So heppy, she rasp song sotto voce
afta I's born . . . see she voce so famous a fable
o myths, even now, samsy, ju can buy her CD
en de world muzak section . . .

Nopullimyuleg, she singsong longest song eva . . .
Sing rasping raus pain . . . mind de gap by way . . .
Hocking, coughing wit one beat
til husking one note . . . con ko bell,
she like a bayou wailer . . .

En stubble field etched by winta's acid light,
she retch her notes . . . y specta's wall o sound
chilled de tympanum o all de saram
who pause, listen, y cry, cry, y cry
fo being a curs'd Korean . . .

Singing while carrying me bundle home,
til I'se a week old, befo she collapse to she death,
she hum her last notes:

A martyr spun nettle out of a silk shorn dress,
A lice-laced boot to my heart in
Angyang I rest . . .

THE LINEAGE OF YES-MEN

Nut'ing but brine jars y jaundice widows en mine old village.
I's come from 'eritage o peddlas y traitors,
whom kneel y quaff a lyre spoon-me-spondas. Mine fadder
sole Makkoli wine to whitey GIs din guidim to widows fo bounce.
Me grandfadder sole Makkoli wine to Hapanese colonists
din he guidim to insurrectas . . . sticka hop? Some pelehuu?

Afta war, villa men pelt mine grandfadder wit ground stones.
He stand in de cold tillim fingas frost jawed, until blewblack.
Villagers callim yellow, callim chihuahua *ssaeki*, a dies irae
fo yesman—he yessed his way to gravestone.

Din mine fadder sole Makkoli—he a 'Merikken GI chihuahua.
Some populii tink GIs heroes wit dim strafing "Pinko chink"
but eh! Those Jees like regula pirates, search for booty y pillage. . . .

He took Jees to war widows tho widows too dry woeing tears
for Eros. He like mine grandfadder yessed y yessed, nodded
til no lift him fes up. In his deathbed . . . sayim to me,
Ttallim, you say no, no, no, you say only no. Him fes
waterlog de liquor y when him die, he retched white.

I join movement to fightim me yesman lineage . . .
Listen to *achim* song . . . woodcut fists lignified
de crowd . . . I fight mine legacy, mine curse
dat pulsed en me aorta to say no. . . .

Note from the Historian
The guide's grandfather was one of the better known *chinalpa* or pro-Japanese collaborators during Japan's colonization of Korea (1910–1945). He was trained as one of the "butchers," amateur guards who rooted out and murdered underground Korean nationalists. But he had a weak stomach and fainted whenever he was near a gutted corpse. So then he made his living selling tips to Japanese officials on the whereabouts of "governments in exile."

THE IMPORTANCE OF BEING ENGLISH

Mine gor-belly fadder a mout-rattla but soma-time
he plant poily bromide in me crania: pep gems dat echo
me mind chamber time y time—*ahar, ahar,*
him saith,

my hut was trampled by American troops,
who turned over barrel wads of cabbages, sticky
red pepper puddles, they spilled everything out

Big booted potato finga'd giants cockim guns
en him ear cos tink he Commie spy. Big error
but all he kaim say? *Ssalyu juseyo!*
Gibberish to dim ears! *Ahar,* him saith,

But then I recognized their translator,
an old school chum. I begged him,
"You know me, why are they doing this?"
He recognized me and took the Officer aside,

and whispered to him in English.
Like a miracle, they rested their guns and walked out the door.

Me fadder sees dis y decide to learn Engrish righteo dere.
Become a Jees cucking stool fo means o survival
me lineage biggum on survival.
'E tell me dis pep gem:

You can be the best talker but no point if you can't
speak the other man's tongue. You can't chisel, con, plead,
seduce, beg for your life, you can't do anything, because you
know not their language. So learn them all.

EXCERPT FROM THE HISTORIAN'S MEMOIR

When I was ten, my father traveled halfway across the globe to help me move in to boarding school. During layover, we sat together in the silent cavity of the airport food court. He swallowed his medication, rasped a sip of his coffee, and then he sighed. He had something important to tell me. I leaned in and he began. When he was young, he could not afford the proper hygiene to care for his teeth. His teeth were so rotten, he had them capped. But he knew that beneath the white enamel sheath, his real teeth hibernated, crooked and stained. He sighed. He feels the deepest shame because of this. He waited for me to respond and when I didn't, he continued. Now that he wasn't around. He coughed and began again. Now that he wasn't around, it is vital that I am responsible for my teeth. He told me of a device called a Water Pik. It has a spigot that squirts a thin pressurized stream of water against your teeth. It acts as a floss but it is more thorough than the (he struggled here for the right word) string floss. He will order me one and have it sent to me immediately. Use it at least three times a day. He gently gripped my arm and added, please.

III

EDUCATION DURING THE YEAR OF FALLING HAIR

EARLY INFLUENCE

Blues mine eyes fade to blues when I's a tot,
mine eyes a blind mon's ghost-oysta eyes,
hair stems prickling out a moonshine crown.

Assim fate flag X mark spot en me,
chillins call me bbak-bbaggi, trow pebbles at mine ball head
while ajamas tut tut, tut tut. Salutations
hab falsetto o "lawdy mine gawd looky dat chile."

Me fadder y I's poor as bats, scab en mine head
frum nits big as O on dis page . . . we eat
glue barley powda som-a-time lardy spice tripe . . .

But mine fadder git Hallmarka cards from Jees.
Gibberish dim greetings since en Engrish grub.
I maki copies bine tracing card onto rice papas wit
pencil stubs . . . gift dim to me classmates,

blues me eyes fade to blues when me a tot,
cos me ball head, dim scorn me see?
I need hip buddy so I bribim . . .

Stops me teacha she sees me she says
"you got betta talent din to hand out de enemy's words. . . ."
She look at card 'sifa toad-spotted, tittled wit pox . . .

I look down at card wim say *Have a Jolly Holiday*:
white hairy fat man in red jogging suit laughim . . .

Dissim be enemy? I ask.
Dissim be enemy, she solemnly said.

CHOLLA VILLAGE OF NO

. . . Progress maif sprinklim fortune
to all o Korea—pave street, condo y petrol
savin Daewoo autos but Progress skip ova mine
villa lika popula lass snubbim
drossy fat girl . . .

. . . villa a sad sack groanim wit bullocks
y huts, villa o exiled outcasts,
prison-loused insurrectas, pickpockets, lady fes
bum-lookas, gaseleo dous'n gun molls,

yam sella clang tin can y hock hot treat
but bine eve, yam sella hatch plan to glue
workas toget'a . . . muckraking strumpets wheedle
tainty secrets from croneymen
who muck dim . . . allatime bang-a-rang,

butchers pang spite fo dim ancestas
macheted fo non bowing too low . . . factory wig
makas paste rash powda onto wigs fo
de sahib patron ladies . . . it be a villa besieged

bine cauldron trouble pot stirrers:
me Cholla villa o no.

But en a villa o contrarians who smelt peppa
gas lika it laughim gas, who quill manifestos
en juice-frail butcher papa, who say no mo, no mo,
no mo, one voice ses hokay, es fine . . .
mine fadder's yes a tic . . .

Mine teacha tell me dat wig-makas
plan to strike . . . see samsy we expoit wigs
to 'Merikken cronettes wit patchy nest hair . . .

. . . (I's a model cos mine ball head, lasses giz me
all de rejects—botchy bleach job wigs,
marcel too knuck-knuck wigs, a nappy wig
fo all occasions). . . .

. . . but hours killim workas, in window black
paint room . . . bone cramp backs en airless room y hack
a lot so plan a mass sit down,
non work til betta pay . . .

I's naifly tellim me fadder . . .
Plis boi patos rush en factory, gets key y squeejee full pow
a hose o wadder . . . hose blast a flood y
shatta workas rib cages, shred de plasta caking
. . . city floatim black balloon . . .

Me gor-belly fadder, de Makkoli bootlegga,
oggled y tattled fo piddling dolla bill . . .
sayim yes, hokay, es fine, tellim secrets. . . .

. . . I'se shame me fadder, I'se shame mefelf,
so I's lefttim en sanguish fog,
I's left me fadder to live wit me teacha.
I ses I go, he non look a'me,
he ses hokay, yes, go.

WINDOWLESS HOUSE

En spitty noon Satriday, we trudged dreaded
Namsan mountain, gamboling past fen y fields whim farmers
en straw chapos picked grinpepas, y past perma
haired ajama who sole fizzy sodas
imported de U.S. o A. . . .

I's clutched a sekrendry source o Marx translated
bine semi-illiterate Korean. A true prole. Many misspellings.
I's a Proles idealologist cos mine teacha.
But she mo cautious din me . . .

She trillt: *If you're caught with that book, they take you
to the windowless house and stab screwdrivers under your nails.*
She maki gesture o dim hypodermically
sticking screwdriva down mine
po' nail. She fright me cos us *on our way*
to windowless house!

. . . fieldtrip to windowless house fo eyeball's load
o 'Merikken puppet plis boi patos'.
This needs to be burned in your memory, she ses. . . .

. . . Cicadas burn en mine ear like *ʒhung, ʒhung.*
A hot hot day. Afta tree mile, we get to
de only Western-style house en villa.

Western-style house where be windows
it be pour concrete. . . .

We hang loose in de bushes . . . I'se sweatim lika madmon
but mine teacha sif pale y dropless.
So bored I'se fallim sleep. Finalmente, door
creaks opens . . .

y rush o rusty wadder flood out de door.
Me teacha breathes. *It's true.* She sayim, *It's true.*
A mon hosing blood out de door. . . .

. . . Later, we find out windowless house
be butcha's house, not plis boi pato's house.
Dim slaughterim pigs . . . but still Namsan
plis boi camp, de whole forest used as engine
to pulp spirit o suspects wit pliers
y batons, de trees rattling not from wind
but cries o mercy.

My father hired a private piano instructor for me in boarding school. She was a middle-aged British woman who lived in an apartment that she furnished with a tweedy, unforgiving sofa and bronze abstracted sculptures that I later realized were imitations of Brancusi. The first day, I gazed at one of the sculptures, marveling at its ugliness, when she asked, "Does it not remind you of a bird?" I nodded although I had no such thought. We finally sat at the piano. To help my fingers curve over the keys, she had my hand piggyback her own hand while she played a simple scale. I rested my hand delicately around her pale, practical hands; her nails were clipped squarely to the quick. She taught me a short rhyme to recite while she played the scale. It was a rhyme to keep one in rhythm: *Peter, Peter Pumpkin Eater, had a wife and couldn't keep her, he put her in a pumpkin shell, and there he kept her very well.* Again and again, she played the five notes while I rested my clammy hand over hers. She insisted that I sing the rhyme with her and I sang along in a voice that was just shy of puberty. I felt like the blind being led like this and I was momentarily aroused.

IV

VISIONS OF
PAMPHLET GODS

SEIZURE

. . . Din she introduce me to Sah,
Sah only one whom din tease me, samsy. . . .
Cos he too chock-a-God as a bwoy . . . too busy
padding to 'im knees y praise-de-Lording as a tot . . .
En school, we learning *ga na da*,
Sah trow backim chair . . .

y collapse hitha y yon . . . Viacles!
'E shaking, tongue roll, chillins cry while him
eyes roll back white, shakishake . . .
Lat'a 'e find he is epilepa . . . but 'e dink 'e got
de God innim, 'e say "I got de God in me!"

Teacha knock sense into him too . . .

But befo teacha knock sense,
Sah's epilepa givem visionaries . . .
putti pink visionaries o lambs mewling
y clouds partim to shine rind o guava light
y hand o God,
lika Sistim chaparel gesture,

dim spirit visionaires stolen right outta pamphlet
pics from Oaklie missionary tub thumpas . . .
him visionaire not origini . . .

But he come to me when we tots 'e say . . .
. . . "Ye eyes like angels blowing dim
glowing bugles . . . ye eyes right outta me
Godly Visionaire" y took mine paw to 'im heart
. . . alis, alas!

. . . When we turn Socialist, 'e hab visionaires
o woodcut serfs rising up, torch to torch,
'e say dis will happen in our nation . . . I say to im,
'his visionare wear falsies, no serfs
en Korea . . .

But yaar, 'e hab point, we grew up
togedda, tarred wit similar brush as dim say . . .
. . . found each ut'a lika two unwanted
lints . . . y physicality, no Don
Ju-yuan . . . our kiss a blotch o two fumbly lips . . .

TIDE POOL

O umbilical blue sea's bob y warble,
en summa's eve, Sah y me scoota'd barnacle
boat off de shores, leaned ova boat's
salt crack rim to lamplight de sea.

We flashlight motion o silva fish swarm,
small as earwigs, fish scittilating en sync,
glinting into mouthing silva auroras,
a shadow flashing o form,

at dawn, Sah bring me ta tide pool . . .
We's squint a' de homestead o gemified fish,
indigo prickle urchins, yeller kiwi sea worms,
flesh tone hermit crabs scrunched into coil shell,
oil wet abalone grip onto moss stone . . .

Mine greedy fingas pry dim all off,
dump en mine bucket . . . Sah ses leavim be,
but I wanted mine own ultra mare tank,
so I'se collectim en mine seawadder bucket . . .

Two days hence, wadder in mine bucket ink rancid black,
hermit crab crawl out its shell floatim up,
sea worm fade fog white, floatim up,
allim die, a dead sea smell
de rank spongim me home.

REUNION

Sah y me ducked into light o mine fadder's home,
where he stooped, frail shirted, mossed en white hair . . .
'E look a'me sifa saw me jus' dat morn,
stead o few year ago, whon I's bindle up
y move to mine teacha's home . . .

. . . bustle en de kitchen y pour us Makkoli,
gib us leatha squid strips so we's sit tacet,
gnaw gnawim on squid strip . . .

Me fadder—a chattabox—hed nut'ing to say,
lung box barrel dry, look bashed as a ch'im spittle salt-sella,
cept 'e say, wit mine new wig, I spittim
image o mine madder,

din he groan outtim chair y needle en a record
o me madder's pansori songs, bend him fes down
to listen she "bestofs," . . .

arrs all bellical! . . . I harrumped out de home wit Sah . . .
I'se sniffed it off . . . hitched onto Sah's bike horns,
We trawl off 'round me old villa . . .

. . . night befo, I's hed terrible dream: an ice storm,
me fadder y me inside a well . . . stuck cos mine head

capped to fadder's head like we simi twins,
swung mine head lika wasp stung bullock . . .

UNIVERSITY YEARS

Him boar-bristle hair, its prickle I usta pat. Stiff hair
means good brawns, Sah yawped. But I'se could
wrastle de bwoy down
in tree minutes flat,

. . . 'Cept in words. We'd trade bawdy élan,
scribble manifestos en nepkins,
stompim hoot matted en passion . . . neat'
bed sheets we a fumblim mess, pray to Priapus,
but in rhetoricism, we ad idem . . .

Which we contrarians reach to lova
spatted pitch, puff-cheeked y red mout'd,
duodene birds pim peck bout ideologems
fo we claud a concialiation . . .

pros y cons of democracy o socialism . . .
. . . pros y cons o Brecht o Beckett, pros y cons
o Beatle o Bobby Dylan (we had issues wit 'Merikkens,
b'we hot-diggity dim rock y roll) . . . I's get so hot,
yearn to stuff his whole being in . . .

. . . Sah's visionaire hike up
to him . . . prophecies mostly garbles . . . he once
say I's be a famed singa like mine madder o 'e ses

dim got a tonic fo me ball head, wait un year . . .
got me hopes up . . .

. . . b'he allatime shaken up 'bout one visionaire,
a shade swallowing de whole city en blood, a riva o carnage,
Army's mandible twain us bloody noon . . .
he ses, intoning lik de Biblical fanatic
he once was . . .

din first shot heard . . . de first shot . . .
Park shot down y Chun du Hwan
took ova—

Oi. Mine voice be hoarse as a crone
o whistlim kazoo . . . I's got to tend to my troat . . .
Limon y wadder is what I's need . . .

I hopped around an archipelago of boarding schools in London, Hong Kong, and Connecticut. School granted me a kind of immunity from my foreign surroundings. School was my embassy. Rarely did I see him except during the yearly holiday reunions, when he would visit *me* (I never returned to Sierra Leone). We would stroll around the empty campus grounds and dine together in a hotel restaurant. He barely aged. His posture remained erect, his hair full and wiry black without a strand of gray. Beyond his yearly visits, he would send me letters that were as terse as Post-it notes tacked onto a refrigerator, always urging me to "Be good! Study hard." In his notes, he would place exclamation points at inappropriate moments: "I work hard everyday!" Never a word about the bloody civil war in Freetown. Never a detailed word about himself. Sometimes he scribbled on a prescription pad, as if he could not be bothered to find a sheet to write on. Although an atheist, he once mysteriously sent me an annotated Bible with a note that said, "Please, put it by your desk! I read it sometimes. Read it when you have the time."

V

INTERMISSION: PORTRAIT OF THE DESERT

ELEGY

Parachute in cloudless cielo und school o jellyfish,
émigrés land in dusty tureen,
and ladled a job
:tram blower,
:jackfruit seller.

ALMANAC

Once, she said this is the way
through the Desert, not to the Desert.

Once, a meteor-mottled terrain,
spotted with buried mines.

Once, hoarding of radios, heard
under blanket mounds.

She warned the adventurer
there were adventurers before him,

Their Desert memoirs never sold,
they drank themselves to sloth.

Once, the Desert was actually a desert.
The guide, the only guide.

*

A honeycomb of lights.
The world pours in.

*

Once, buried mines, leftovers of war.
Many locals had missing limbs.

They adapted, created a caste system:
the fully limbed down to the fully limbless.

One intermarriage:
A wedding with bowls of expensive oranges.
The bride in a kelly green shawl,
her long, elegant arms draped around
the limbless groom.

*

They now live where the mines sleep.
They look iris-to-knothole
into the city of too many lights.

ALMANAC

Blood tone   flood tone
woods over-swarmed with description
starless   riotous   woods

writhing not with wolf nor lion.
Writhed with guides who emerged
with their chromatic lore

paved arteries   hotels   grease-shined
with locals   we guide   guide
I am crammed with tongues   crammed

with guides who ache for their own
guides   who mourn   who lead
men from human rinds of discontent,

shuttle   mutiny   *stench and swelter*
aborigine who leads vested men through
stream snake   brush   who gust

shave your hair   ulcerate your nemesis
guide to spectral love   to animal behavior
to coitus in a hot tub

a cherry tour bus skidded   overturned
travelers shimmied out in droves while
inflammable gases blushed out

fish lens porn   bushel of mustard spices
2nd world auto dealers   rotisserie roar
of champagne volcanoes

I paddle down the bodies with an oar's
thwack   the storage of migrants kept
under   gouting   stream

Is that gun fire? Rat-a-tat?
What cadaverous blooms?   Faces smear
against my windshield   crying

we will tar you with birds
succor soon   yassir   a fleet of skiffs
zigzag paths   look here to sylvan arroyo

flattened tonsil   woods break off
into series   coma
oh radiant lives

all guides
all beautiful   erroneous
unison.

ALMANAC

Like Penelope weaving   unweaving
they've crossed   recrossed
over the steel corseted bridge

to unfractured idiom. Ah! No longer
the tongue anahems with another
man's slangy ahems,

dander dregs of their mynah bird's
trill sloughs into river's trough.
A monologue distilled   shrilled

exiled, they cross the ratcheting bridge.
Their ribbon of clocks rattling tick,
belted around their waists.

O leather river beds, potted with
wells of water, potted with bombs,
how this bridge looms over you.

One-way pass for them with their
dungarees of keyhole locks.
It is not etiquette the way they hold on,

the way their necks twist back, singing
origin, la la. The way they rub their whittled
idols inside their shawls so they catch fire,

how they frisk their heads around
when they hear the shots, but see,
those shots are not for them.

A lot nearby, a man whose job
it is to put to rest greyhound dogs
too slow for the track.

Succumb he says   the dog succumbs.
Cradle its deer-like head   whisper a prayer
into the dog ear's felt   and aim.

ALMANAC

Toward this pale-mouthed popping light,
exiled rooks pearled with the self-same
gene, sneak back toward

mosquito wraithed, bombarded air
fueled by carbon gasps of men
bobbing in manmade canals, toward

hotels of white watted carapace,
hotels of watered sward, waddled orchids,
hotels of exterminated scorpions,

and enact the role of seers, dancing a toll,
a toll, misguiding travelers to stumble
into mines from last era's war,

diagram's anagram of its radiant
aim, opal ruptures in milky air,
cameo effects to sampled song,

rended travelers are tissues wrestling
in flame, blasts in this guttering dawn,
this spittle of unrest,

lovely day, lovely day now
says the rabid girl and nips
at a sun-seared hand.

NEW TOWN

Architecture
They demolished all the ghost towns and consolidated them into high-rise apartments made of poured concrete. Like Le Corbusier's Notre Dame du Haut, each window is cut like a musical note on a score. But the windows are narrow, allowing only a fleck of light.

Population
Grows each time Desert officials exile natives to New Town: a guide, a hotel maid, a street vendor who sells off-season fruit, an engineer of bombs.

Borders
The border moves a quarter of an inch east everyday, and so imperceptibly, that natives do not notice until suddenly a clothesline is over so that they must retie the clothesline.

Language
First began warping when the first ship docked and they hybridized a word for money so that group 1 would understand group 2. But in New Town, there is not a trace of trade here. They can follow their words back to the first tribe.

Disease
One man watched two boxers. He recalled one boxer making a shot-gun left jab. The second boxer taking the hit. He recalled jeering. He recalled craning his neck and squinting for a better view. Then the boxers dissolved. He recalled seeing only their sweat-washed contours and the shudders in the air from their phantom sparring. Every three minutes, the bell clanged for rest and there were no bodies, and then there was no ring, and then he recalled, there was nothing.

Photos
New Town is without image. It cannot be imagined.

Religion
They rub their mouths along a stone until chapped skin bursts to blood.

Landmark
The bridge spans from a coronary of streets to corpses white lime.
The bridge spans over riverbed vanishing into riverbed.
As exiled natives cross, they turn their heads so far back, their heads seem wired backwards, as if frozen in a paralytic fit. Tears trail down to the clefts of their asses. Even their sadness absurd.

Law
Is the sin of choice.

Jobs

Desert officials raided one room, slit open a boy's belly to see if he stored land mines in his body. Afterwards, the father suffered hysterical blindness. His other son snuck back into the city to assume the role of guide.

Nomenclature

Travelers are not allowed to visit New Town.

Resources

In a river by one hotel, he guided three tourists on a sampan boat with a blood orange sail, stern oar to sludge green water. Letheward, he led them, out the boat, leading them with a chatter of invention, down to the riverbeds pocked with mines. Three explosions wisped white gowns in the air. He came back home alone to New Town.

EXCERPT FROM THE HISTORIAN'S MEMOIR

I was not allowed into the streets of Sierra Leone so I drew my own. A city where ice stairways spiraled from Prussian blue palaces and roller-coaster tracks wound through a stranger's bedroom, out the window and dropped like a barometer in the coldest winter day. But I was a poor illustrator. The world was crystallized in my mind but I could only manage box-like houses and crooked roads. As I tried to etch the friezes of heroes in their chariots, my waxy crayon leaked dull squiggles. So my childish draftsmanship forced me to focus on smaller things. I drew the key that unlocked the chapel of canary yellow glass. I drafted the first step to a helically shaped staircase at the bottom corner of a paper. "It is a button," I explained to my puzzled father as he examined a penciled dot, the only mark on the paper. "A button that you press. If you press it, it will open doors to a soaring birdhouse so all the birds can swoop in."

VI

RESUMING THE DESERT TOUR: TOWARD THE OUTSKIRTS, TOWARD THE BRIDGE

BASEMENT OF THE ST. PETERSBURG HOTEL

Samsy! D'yer see film comedy?
A marchy band right-o-way make wrong turn, astray
from ticka-tape parade into dead end alley,
y blindly tooting brass coronets, *crash-boom-bang*
into brick wall: trombone, tuba y all
dat brass cymbaling into cacaphonics . . .

We dead end. Les' turn back. . . .

Arise from intestinal runnels y chambas,
we bat we eye hairs to wan open light. Here too dim.
Dead scald world full o rust puddles, grim service men,
y ffyurious mekkinations,
bosh dis stygian hush, bituminely I'se reflect . . .
'Nuff storypipim bout Korea! Factum est,
bio is done. We flee dis hotel,

Head to riva shore mobbled wit clacking oystas
glazed wit silk mud. We grab one, shuck silva gut,
de mind un isle, de body happily fed.

MUSIC OF THE STREETS SERIES

1. HAGGLERS IN THE BAZAAR

Odes scuppa off lika fat wingless birds
from hum-a-day coralim streets.

Hurdy-gurdy sounds: cricket shrieks
o mahikit, abraded music slum scent.

How-kapow pops, a lime streak starled
lika Gerty's bloomas fire crack de dusky violet sky.

Glaceed maple swine sole en street,
now'n we' gwon y eat it, wit one dolla dolla beer.

Gash o Gar. It be de sound o dumb person.
Pay no mind. Gash o Hoi. Oi! It be beat box

o radish mon, one bushel o dim bitta root.
Und dot. A drunk swags a bilish song,

Greps poetica—"Oh Mary O'Doule,
don't make me a fool, turn me into a man anew."

Tink y *tank* y *tunky-tunk-tunk.*

2. THE HULA HOOPER'S TAUNT

I'mma two-ton spiker   hips fast rondeau
n'ere more nay sayer   feel this orbit rattle

Wipe that prattle that spittle   crass pupa
gupta   away you   ma' man,

where you   revolving   solving
spin shorty   shark   satellitic   fever

leer not, lyre   I spiral atom pattern
faster than you say my turn.

Note from the Historian
We wandered into a stadium where thirteen hundred people competed for the
national hula hooper's contest. The last one standing won the contest. While
hula-hooping, they taunted their neighbors to discourage them. From your
seats, you could not actually hear them but I snuck onto the grounds where I
overheard the invective. I also enjoyed sitting high up on the bleachers to lis-
ten to the deafening rattle of thirteen hundred hula hoops in action.

3. THE AUCTIONEER'S WOO

First up is a mint, a classic:
May I have this dance: a phrase for thy empire
waisted who know the finickeries and fineries
of a pearl, small and mottled as a current.
A fetish for yore, when ladies sat by
wayside while side burned men in frippery
whispered an ear-shaped *shall*. Gay buyers,
This is a proper woo, a very proper woo, with
societal promises of velvet crushed cossets
and a lock of Anglophine hair as keepsake,
when joy, now ineluctable as waltz, was
momentary surrender and not a holiday
reminder. Here here, for those who pang
for manners, who will by code fan gnats
from a sylph's bosom, yet dare not touch
Her pomegranate lips—use it sparingly,
this phrase's hoary delicacy may fray with
slattern use: Come all, for this mint:
May I have this dance!
The bidding will start at once.

Note from the Historian
We were at the auctioneer's tent where trademarks are auctioned off every
week. In the Desert, so many words have become trademarked that it is impos-
sible to even speak without stumbling upon someone's trademark.

4. DANCE HALL SONG FOR WHEN YOU'RE IN THE MOOD

She a swift fire cat bristlin' she fie

She a clean rifle in bombo red car

She a gimme agony 'hind a meat shed

She nuzzle me pizz I nick her bat bat

She a illywacka she swipe a me cash

She a kingpin she sing orda o de Keys.

She a keen song summa sound sea.

Note from the Historian
Dance hall stalls are located at the end of the bazaar. Stall after stall, there is a
different deejay but with the same soundtrack of the sea. While some, like this
stall, are humble tents with a sandy floor, two turntables, and a mic, a few other
stalls are warehouse-sized affairs with a 27,000-watt sound system and official
greeters who hand you swim caps as you enter the front door.

5. TOASTS IN THE GROVE OF PROPOSALS

Lo, brandied man en rabbinical cape
dab rosy musk en goy's gossamy nape,
y brassy Brahmin papoosed in sari's saffron sheet
swoon bine faire Waspian en 'im wingtip feet,
les' toast to bountiful gene pool,
to intramarry couple breedim beige population!

Lo, union o husky Ontarian y teacup size Tibetan,
wreath en honeysuckle y dew-studded bracken,
lo, union o Cameroon groom kissim 'e gallic Gamine's cheek
en miscegenatin' amour dim seem to reek
les' toast to bountiful gene pool,
to intramarry couple breedim beige population!

Clap away, Greek chorus o gay sashayim crowd,
clap away, chatty flackmen y pre-nup hackmen,
bine fort, ruby-lined pachyderms who trundle here proud,
bine fort, madders who nag fo proposal enactment,
les' toast to bountiful gene pool,
to intramarry couple breedim beige population!

O LIGHT, RED LIGHT

Girls! Girls! Girls! Batted eyelashes at boned molish chap,
but like Greco Frieze, him stood en cold puddle o red light,
spite one Girl! curdling she finga, "*Come bwoy, Come, don' g'won.*"
Toto sum Girls! curdled fingas attim but he maki no choice.
Only browsed y sighed "'nut'a day." Went back, spillim seeds
onto hotel carpet, lone, wit only zuzzing cable, a suite nocturne.

Ai fife, he warbled, Ai la lune triste nocturne.
Him capered down to karaoke lounge to sing, a sloshing chap,
at hotel, quaffing Singapore Slings wit pomegranate seeds.
Next day, 'e kem back to Girls! to fes de garnet light.
Fished outtim haisimap pinga, but brined bine choice
'e sterilized, y Girls! chortled "*G'won home, batty bwoy, g'won.*"

'Im moist eyes be anime anemone, he g'won
back, pining Don Ho's "Tiny Bubbles," a blarny mon nocturne.
'Im catcha "desertitis." "*The sensation of feeling deserted after
   facing too many choices.*"
Infectim neurotic forest like SSRI pips: him pinga all chap.
So, return to him hum-a-day life, to fes domicile's wan light
dreamim o him beer comrades belly laugh attim wasted seeds.

Ai, wine o consciousness fermented from brain's wadder, what seeds
sprout in de desert? We labor por him joy. Neva we g'won.
Nary, we work ovatime, shaving de tourist's cuticle til dead o light.

Crooning wit our ragged troats de 99th nocturne,
but, you, non! Begum tourists cannot be slaked, troats chap
lika duck wit chokelace dat cannot feast en fish o choice

We offal de finest sampla, a bouquet o choice,
but desertitis cankas digestion, whateva you've see'd
yea desire reined, saddled like apaloosa horse's leatha chap.
He wit rattled mind, slumped home to Jersey, from desert he g'won!
En 'im suit attire, 'e whom cannot be sated, snored nocturnes
en 'im town's train station tru eve's descending light.

Fraid o failure, fraid to fes wife en halogen light,
act o returning a requiem, neva a choice,
but dawn's aubade caressim prickle cheek, singing away nocturne.
Though banished, he can come back to him life, begin afresh, aseed,
tourist's privilege be dat he can return, always return, though
    frum desert he g'won.
"Wake up, ole chap, wake," a janitor clap in 'im ear til janitor
    hands all chap.

Eye-crust y feral mout, 'e wink awake to janitor's flashlight.
A pitiable chap but hab choice to g'won home, I's covet dat choice.
When dim ideas seed in us, how do we'um return, when we can
    only g'won.

ONCE THE FACTORY, NO LONGER THE FACTORY

Remain o last factory . . .
A carp cannery worst idea eva, tourists wanna carp fish
en lily pond not en dim soup, yaar . . .

Workas usta embalm fish meat wit preserves,
punch-im-in cans y expoited out cans
to collect dust en supa-mahikets en de "Asia"
section, beside can litchi nut . . .

Since n'won eat de cans, caveat emptor, no pickled
chicken o sea dis carp . . . feedim to service louts like mefelf
y whon we shun it, feedim to jailbirds who
bang-a-rang trew a riot afta spot can-juice fish
on dim tin dented trays . . .

Now, gaggle o carp en 20,000 fountains,
tang-color fish o Hapanese gentility groomed
bine pro Osakan carp caretakas en tang-color jumpsuits,
. . . Some pelehuu? . . . sticka hop?

Nomono factory, nary a gewgaw screwed
en bine clouts wearim hair net y saran-wrappy gloves,
here no mo, now all customa is king service . . .

Les go, I'se pesky phobic. . . .
Some-a-time, I'se feel lika fish en wadder balloon,
fightim rubber confines, thrashim tail 'gainst stretchy walls . . .
little wadder y non oxygen,
slowly expiating . . .

THE GUARDSMAN'S WARNING

lest ye covet a forkin sinus punch on ye gob, cargo on,
lest ye old cheek wants a bing cherry shine,
cargo on, get off ye sprakin dunghill pulpit
cork ye hole, I'll swipe ye lilliput
double-A sized boom box,
give it 'ere, lest ye tip me a cheroot
to puff, din smack ye lung trap,
get on, nu'ting to see . . .

Note from the Historian
Guardsmen in long black coats spiraled around the bridge that led to New
Town, warding off trespassers and curiosity seekers. One of them attempted to
hustle us away, but then there was a blast, another landmine accident, and all
the guards rushed off toward the smoke.

THE BRIDGE

... Do not trust hidebound jingo-purists,
origini tippa-me turbans, exiled o'er bridge
to ciudad borders, who allatime sneak
back miming as guides ...

Follow dim, you get spulched ... dim will say
"Visit emeril fields, kept alive b'our
state-o-de-art sprinkler system ..."
Ka-pow!

Pied pipers lead ye to dunes liced wit land mines
dat slice all ye limbs off ... no waltzing, no jiggying
afta dat yaar, be a spoonfed basket case ...
Ai, a pis pis life ... so, watchela!

... you neva know who's who ... mingle like
shadows en populii, I's could be dim ... ha ha,
laugh out loud, kay? I's not be dim, otherwise
you's hobblim wit no leg b'now ...

... ai, as aborigini exiled to terra new town,
molecule up to one corp ... dim will
try to wrest desert back ... feisty mongas
dim are ... rise up like an arkpeelago o corks
in sea like de last time,

day o dance dance revolution . . . no relation
ta Hapanese dance game . . . ipso facto no dancing
eider in de revolution. . . .

. . . I's love mine vocation cos mine fat fingas squished
in all pie fruit filling . . . b'needs to rake profit,
samsy, tourism not so hop now . . .

So I'se spy en spies fo a buck,
tip Desert officials whom raid jingo-purist hovels
y haulem off to camps . . .
Needs it samsy, fo me retirement fund . . .

D'wan stare at me, I usta be jingo-purist mefelf!
A fist-a-cuff naysaya! Now I'm nut'ing but a yeller
cawin' castrati, wire-tappim for pennies . . .

Sah'd be shamed, me spyim like dis . . . see I imagine
Sah was dead befo ye come here to bug me,
imagine he died en de blast en Kwangju . . .

I even saw 'im shade. . . .

. . . bine night, eddyim puddle 'neat de bridge
a mud soaked head pops up y stare up,
it be hissim a'me "Shame, shame . . . !"
Is it mine fes reflected, is it Sah stuck in stream?

. . . I's not miming as guide, but I wait
like mines napping in sand,
I wait . . .

For several months, I went to a military school in a tiny city that dissolved in its own quagmire. It was a barrack of a school house surrounded by five hundred flags painted in violent sunsets. I used to escape to a lake black as squid ink, where lamps floated like candle-wicked bowls along water's tremors. Here, the only evidence of the city's torn carapace and its hundred little fires was a radio's isolated squalls. I would be belly up in water, breath rasping in my ears, beetles skating orbits as I stared at the sun shedding itself. Once, I was caught deep in the radish fields, burning ants with a magnifying glass. I was forced to bow before each flag. The cicadas electrified, my wool blazer was swamped with sweat, as I bowed and bowed. I sang a song of beautiful obscenities out of earshot while I bowed before each flag. And then I had to do it all over again, the bowing, until the school house emptied, and the teacher shuffled his papers into his bag and worriedly touched his tumor behind his ear, and the sun dipped over the horizon, and all there was, was my breath.

VII

KWANGJU

ELEGY

Awaken, bull-finch, your noon blink readily. I node ye
noon-time, noon. Awaken, ye left me slurred, tongue still bobbed,
robbed of pullet sun, me wig one dread knot
from sand dune's shoulder, noon

lashed shut, knotted dots dim horizon,
I ye trebled chill betwixt, if a flood in desert dread,
ire water's rush, ire swamps gambler's flush,
I plunge water's surface and look noon,
look, for the cold meat
of your hand.

THE VOICE

*

. . . Dim call me voice o Kwangju,
uprising's danseur principal . . . but samsy, es funny,
I's voice o Kwangju since dim multitudes who
cryim fo acceptance shun mine presence . . .

. . . I's lose me wig en passion o rally,
mine ball head nekked, mine oysta eyes
filla-up wit wadder, stompim podium,
spout ricanery to rally crowd . . .

. . . but crowd dim boo me, t'row rocks a'me,
rocks intended fo plis boi patos, balfastards, trown a'me!
So I's paddles tru clog, aways from Sah, run
y hide en me dead fadder's house, hid like
I's hidim now en Desert . . .

*

. . . Bine day tree o aataclap, heads lop off,
bung it up union leadas 'rrested, bayoneted,
teacha celled fo espyim, pulp students
slung into trucks lika spud sacks . . . no leaders
left . . . Sah ask please come back,
we's need direction . . .

I slink back, no heraldic air . . .
. . . No trumpetim angel me am from 'im visionaire. . . .
Bitta I's am, not wantim to fes n'won . . .
Sotto voice I's ses to Sah, I's don want to
fes n'won. . . .

. . . Sah ses kay, you'll fes n'won b'gib dim
ye voice . . . pirated a notch en radio
fo me . . . aways from batons, de scourgim
eyes . . . en me amprage
hole, I's shotput mine
nihilent gallicry . . .

Mine voice chattel tru amps, transista radios,
clock radios, furred mine voice tru batta'd Kwangju
streets, while mine scolded ball head
cloaked deep en broom sweepa closet wit mike . . .

. . . Hearim me voice en radio, ma che si,
pot-belly war veterans sling up
WWII carbine rifle gainst sifa tanks . . . Coal miners
donated dim detonatas . . . Housewives fed scabbard insurrectas
wit hot bowls o *ttok-guk*. . . .

. . . Steetwalkas hear me y march to hospital
to donate blood . . . haggard doctas say no!
to torn-stock streetwalkas who kem to donate
she blood but dey yell, "Our blood is clean too!"
while beatim dim chest . . .

. . . Paratroopa clip off amp wires
but Mr. Cha come y rewire
amp back . . . mine decibel swatted away dragonflies
swarmim round shredded bodies . . . cut tru smoke
y copsal stink, clear eyesights
sored from peppa gas . . . lorn in lore o love . . .

b'all ended . . . paratroopas find where we be,
surround de school basement . . . try to smoke
us out into rancid air . . . I's first to
sneak out back way . . . paratroopas
rushed into school . . .

while I's rush away, t'inkim Sah behind me . . .

I's plunged inta frail ragged mob, who
gib me a kerosene bomb to hit de school . . .

. . . Shroud o gnats in late aftanoon sun,
shroud o mob

A frail body o toweled mob
bull-dozed one afta mob
into mob into   frail body o
toweled mob   dove sta memora

I trew

. . . a kerosene bomb, it twine en air
a kerosene bomb roll, it twine en air,

did not soar as I's plan   but
float, but before plummet before
spume gown o powda
I replay dat arc intra air, tortuously
twist as I's look befo fleeing,
will it hit its target is Sah out
is Sah out is he
y replay.

KWANGJU REPLAYED

... ghouls,
chewas o corpse en gear. . . . See dis?
Scar from paratroopa pistol whip
me 'til I saw mine dead madder wave from putti pink
skies . . . want some tea? some pelehuu?

... plum blossoms float en hair   cicada
ring . . . Gumnamro swelled wit broomsweepas
contractas, Koh's wife who work *tok-guk* stand y pop
Koh's zits en front everyone . . . Nation swelled wit'out AP . . .
. . . sticka Hop? Exotic as sticka Wrigley . . .

... lika lady liberty from Tinny-man, I was mascot
cos me ball head, me haole eyes . . . a dark cantata rose
geared cockchafas stood en alarum . . . you 'fraid
what I say? Good. . . . I led de cantata . . . de chant I did yes.
I was mascot . . .

... whistles, a flute rust of oil pool y arms,
arms! . . . Sah say stand en pedestal to inspire de crowd.
I say naw. Want to join crowd pie . . . befo pie spit en me
cos me winebig oysta eyes y me ball head . . . now me fes in
all de postas . . . know me nation biggest export o
human hair wig? . . . haha

. . . tea? some pelehuu? Whistle a flute rust o oil
pool y arms raised . . . me troat rust . . .
Aime, I said to dim, you louse, beat it, I despise de flunkies o order
evil gri, mites of a petty monk . . . stool of a flea-bitten
donkey . . . we

hailing y railing, we hailing y railing . . .

. . . Centipede o batons irrigated de crowd,
leaving blood marsh . . . volt shields pool . . . mine
arm flat de floor de feet . . . tied back wit wire . . .
me fes down smelling jellied fluid . . . Dam bladdabags
blew . . .

De blood marsh spread . . . 'tho we faitim
. . . de blood marsh spread . . .
Hop? Desert's finest . . .

. . . ran into amperage church
where pink-eyed cowlies shooed y tinctured. . . .

. . . Metal scrolled ova stores, nu'tting open . . .
ran inside bus as centipede lashed ova Gumnamro . . .
. . . arms, de flute rust arms . . . stamen up heliotropes
shot dead . . . seismic flute shrilled fo citron tanked throng . . .
. . . Sah burn in de gri corona or was it mine . . .
mine fault? . . .

mine fault
me light der color of *bokum* . . . arms,
Sah de last throng I held . . .
Before I sunk . . .

YEARS IN THE
GINSENG COLONY

. . . lush sybaritic hills y allatime sun
spin me into wowow pamphlet whence hard labor
chicanery, bogus as dial-a-phone . . .
work was ginseng, de herb dat maki men testes
balloon . . .

. . . wine pink dawn we pick ginseng
from mossiest soil . . . we hurl en wheel barrow we so
hungry, we ate bugger critter, we gag from allatime singing *Ai*
in hintry field when piss bag guard
plug out dead's meteor socket . . . mine fes scallop
wit dung britter fleas . . .

. . . we suck dew when tongue dreck dry . . . we pick so
spine pulse ppalge plum . . . one ajossi hab closet full o
corn pip fo rat trap to make rodent jerky . . . If no meat
en bone we get blista yello eye . . . once ova dere

I's sees mine teacha, mine teacha whom I's
not seen for year . . . she five stone lighta . . . I turn on her
dere, ses I've learn nut'ing but pain, nomo pain, if I escape
Dis dreadnaught, only pleasure from n'won . . .

I wake en de fog like fizzy alka-selza descend down
en de emeril mountain en I sigh,

fo its beauty . . . Bulching out me sockets
were tears when dim close dat inferno

. . . vivliacal viasis! I hed too many close ones
die en dere wit oil clod en dim talk hole, skewered to dead wit
rod . . . but no mo, none . . . Now I guide like leading gnu
   clittering down knoll though me
accent come go like cuckaholding hussy. . . .

Note from the Historian
Once, I traveled to South Korea and visited the gulag that has now been con-
verted to, ironically, a slaughterhouse. They took me on a brief tour through
the plant. At one point, I peeked inside one small vestibule on the third floor
and found this inscription:

1. I wake up. I breathe. I leap.
2. I wake up. I breathe.
3. Oranges. When was the last time.
4. How to lay hands on the loved one.

VIII

DANCE DANCE

ELEGY

Such poisonous families
I startle. *Alarum*, the feudal world.
Plow the oil rig and plum blossom fields, the fields where they
danced half-ring,
the aorta mortuary fields. The fields. If not for
the field here, there are
animal wanderings.

My father watched he watched
outside the window he saw he saw
the comet streak klieg light the setting light the world parcels off
into mindless.
Trees in essence flagrant assonance
I suck back into my mouth.

I am this chair, talking to him,
if the burden is to go back.
The world parcels off into seepage, capillary tea bags he said,
he said I must work, I said
I had no dreams that night.
But allure the shoe-polished twilight,
brunt flotilla of stars

this minus store amid the fields,
amid the blight amid

the cold ball bearing I yearn,
for you who lastly fueled breathing this air this air.

ORPHIC DAY

. . . Whon crayfish red sun pop
y electricians drop dead, so string lights
are night twigs en dune chafe wind . . .

. . . whon invocations misfired
so birdcallas attracts mosquitos,
y lovelorn Balladeers incite Brueglian mobs . . .

. . . whon a guide loses sense y drag tourists
down eyeless tour til trapped
en marsh's eye-snappim reeds . . .

. . . we float like incubated bodies,
cranial nerves pulse violet, fire tinsel out
we poppy seed eyes, deep en brine solution,
we blubba our slattern dreams.

THE REFINERY OF VOICES AND VICES

. . . D'yea sees it, yonda ova bridge,
d'yea sees de smoke curdlim air ova slag
limestone tureen. . . .

. . . All's I do is wait, dim 'ready
planned a blast coronal, clotting toget'a,
sabotage is pending, soon ye scat now
o ye be . . .

. . . bombing de impostring,
miming guides plotting, potting more mines,
hatching en gunny sack houses, anecdote
will come a momentum . . .

. . . rushing, rushing onward
salvi facti sunt humming will louden,
heighten wit durable actions . . .

. . . a silence to crave, not dis babel,
a sly unrest, a sly darting dance, no delightful
marches fo mo dreadful measures . . .

. . . I's unpeel mine insides fo one clean note
tru all de marshy crowd sounds, tru all de trademark
cowed libel, I's unpeel mefelf lika pin-hole
neck sweater . . .

. . . guides sidelimned, but b'night a fusion,
trickling back, dartim past bridge whiles
guards be asleep, whiles tourists
be tipplim . . .

. . . drain y damp o quality o life,
o desert, sweep unda bridge, dim guides sweep
unda storyline, sweep unda you,
soaking into tureen lotted plot . . .

. . . I's sum o all I's rued, sum o me accents
y twill mine worn, travels mine tilled, deaths mine endured,
Sah I's left y Sah you've brung beck,
'e's allatime dead to me, 'e's yours yours,
caesuras slicing mine dialect,
Dim measure me skull, I say stop measuring my skull . . .

. . . Summon mine last sieved blood
invocation det roused tousands not fluke
o me guided flute which led you
to dis mine pocked river, sum me might
so I's be righted . . .

Might I brush out dragonfly wings
from mine wig.
If de world is our disco ball,
might I have dim dance.

EXCERPT FROM THE HISTORIAN'S MEMOIR

It was his day off. My father stayed home. He took his medication and placed a jam jar on the windowsill and studied the jar against the landscape. He remembered the touch of an old lover's hand against his coarse wiry hair. He gave himself four minutes to think about Sujin. He had that gift, or neurosis, to set time limits on his daydreams, as if his reflections were naps. He set these time limits, sometimes going so far as to set an alarm clock, so that he wouldn't sink into that *state*. A shot. He started. Then he slumped back against the chair by the windowsill. The civil war died down but there were still his patients with pains from their phantom limbs. There was still the occasional unrest. The jar, with the clear raised glass logo of *Holly's Preserves*, reflected light and framed the landscape before it. Slowly his head lolled back against the chair. He fell asleep. The jar clear yet moted with dust, contained the front yard and the sapling, the rusted iron gate and beyond it a horizon. A puff of smoke. Beyond the iron gate, the horizon, grains of salt enlarged to a crowd that filled the frame of the jar. He woke up and took off his glasses. Unmindful of any sound, he fell back asleep.